Canoodle Marketing
Creating Customer Loyalty
& Building Your Brand

By Dennis Regling

www.canoodlemarketing.com

The Author
"Mr. Dennis"
Dennis Regling

4

Terms and Conditions

LEGAL NOTICE

The Publisher has strived to be as accurate and complete as possible in the creation of this report, notwithstanding the fact that he does not warrant or represent at any time that the contents within are accurate due to the rapidly changing nature of the Internet.

While all attempts have been made to verify information provided in this publication, the Publisher assumes no responsibility for errors, omissions, or contrary interpretation of the subject matter herein. Any perceived slights of specific persons, peoples, or organizations are unintentional.

In practical advice books, like anything else in life, there are no guarantees of income made. Readers are cautioned to reply on their own judgment about their individual circumstances to act accordingly.

This book is not intended for use as a source of legal, business, accounting or financial advice. All readers are advised to seek services of competent professionals in legal, business, accounting and finance fields.

You are encouraged to print this book for easy reading.

Table Of Contents

Foreword

Though lead generation for business purposes can be a rather daunting task, there are various simple ways that can be adopted to keep the exercise as simple as possible. This time tested methods have proven to be very useful for those attempting the further their business forays or expand current business opportunities.

As well, customer loyalty is the single most important element to retain within a business relationship. A lot of positive elements can be derived from a well established loyal customer base. Huge amounts of money is periodically allocated to advertising, primarily to garner a bigger market share of consumers, but with the existence of a loyal customer base, this expenses can be channeled towards other better and more beneficial areas.

Get And Keep Customers

Chapter 1: *The Basics*

Synopsis

Lead generation is popularly used as an effective tool to generate the necessary interest or inquiry into products or services of any particular business listing. This tool is particularly useful for the internet marketing platform where is can be utilized to garner a larger list of customer information such as list building, e-newsletter list acquisition or for the simple method of winning customers.

As well, companies which have a satisfactory percentage of loyal customers have the advantage of channeling funds into a self reinforcing system in which the company delivers constantly evolving superior value and high quality products and services.

This will further create the comfortable relationship desired to continue to successfully keep the customers both happy and loyal.

There is also the added advantage of the preexisting customers who consciously help to introduce friends and family to consider using the products and services based on personal testimonies and enthusiasm.

The Basics

Though seemingly similar to advertising, the lead generation can at most time be almost generated from non paying sources predominantly garnered from search engine results or referrals from an existing customer base.

Taking the trouble to research the needs and interest of the potential customers targeted often helps to narrow down the lead generating tool to better attract the attention and commitment of the potential customer.

Once this vital information is formatted then the service or product that is being fielded will be better received by its target audience. Using this tool to set up seminars and webinars can also be a great way to attract the attention of the customer base especially if the topics hosted are both interesting and informative.

Adding the interactive feature would also help to ensure the participation of the target audience for further enhancement of information vital to the success of the product or service being launched.

The lead generation tool is predominantly meant to enhance or even take the business foray to a whole other level and thus should be explored, as its benefits are no doubt beneficial and most times positive.

As well, retaining loyal customer ratios at an all time high lies in the fact that companies are able to focus on providing good customer induction schemes that contribute to a higher yielding customer base and thus provide for higher profits by reducing the need to spend money attracting potential but not necessarily viable customers. However, such schemes should in no way take the place of good and resoundingly exemplary customer service.

The element of trust is rather hard to accomplish and even harder to nurture, but with the right daily process in place and use without deviation it is very possible to build the desired trust factor between both parties.

This trust factor will then translate to converting the casual customer into a loyal one. Thus, any complaints or misgivings regarding the products or services should be addressed swiftly and to the satisfaction of the customer. Companies that take the grievances of a customer seriously are usually the ones that have the highest loyal customer base on record.

Chapter 2:

*Provide Value And Figure Out Where Y
our Customer Loyalty Is*

Synopsis

With the variety of products and services available in the market place today being so vast, it is sometimes difficult to get the desired attention of the already greatly shrinking customer base.

Being able to discern one's position with regards to the customer loyalty ratio can be rather tricky if not virtually impossible sometimes. However thankfully there are some tried and true methods that can be used to achieve this goal.

Where Is It

To create the scenarios to further snag and keep the customers loyalty can be an ever stressful ongoing challenge. Thus there is a need to explore in-depth and seriously consider the needs and wants of the anticipated target audience to ensure continued success.

Taking the extra measure to provide the target audience with the necessary assurance of supply value is perhaps a platform that should be given due consideration.

Building relationships that promise the interest of the customer would be of foremost consideration is one way to create the supply value ratio. When a customer is made to feel important the loyalty factor which is necessary for repeat sales is evident. Randomly using methods that don't include this vital and necessary element is both unwise and can be rather costly.

As the lead generation tool can be used for almost any business foray, the customer base that can be garnered is indeed huge and thus ensuring the supply value angle is thoroughly covered within this tool is not only beneficial for both parties but also ensure the interest of the potential customer from the onset of the introduction.

From the potential customer's point of view the supply value should include various different initial vital information such as pricing, product quality and capabilities, availability, after sales services and any other potentially perceived useful information. Providing the potential targeted customer with such information will also help to plant the seed of confidence in the company and product being presented.

Including other added value features is also another way to enhance the product or service, as this would also be perceived as supply value for the customer.

Being able to retain a loyal customer base has its merits and understanding the customer sentiment is pivotal to achieving this loyalty factor.

As loyal customers are a good indicator to a thriving and consistently successful business endeavor, taking the time to focus on understanding the level of each customer's loyalty is both prudent and beneficial in the long term state.

This understanding can help predict to a certain extent the ratio between the potentially loyal customer and those who may not ever become the desired loyal customer needed to keep the business a success.

By making this discovery the company can then take the necessary action to try to prevent potential customers from just being one time users.

Some things to seriously consider in the quest to understand the company's position within the customer's mindset would be as follows:

• Making the effort to gather the required data to assess the potential customer's reason for making the purchase or for showing an interest in the service or product offered.
• Finding out if the customer would be willing or even happy to introduce the product or service to others.

• Getting feedback of the level of satisfaction derived from using the product or the lack of said satisfaction. Armed with this information, there should also be a proactive counter action to address any negative feedback learnt.

• With the information gained from the customers, there should be a concerted effort to make the necessary improvements to the products or services to further encourage the commitment on the part of the customer to stay loyal

Chapter 3:
What People Need

Synopsis

To a certain extent perceptions are made based on the knowledge garnered through specific means. However these means and methods may not always be reliable thus creating the possibility of ineffective handling of any problems or needs that may arise. For any product or service to become a success and sustain itself there is a definite advantage to understanding the target audience and their needs.

With every venture undertaken, the most dominant feature desired would be to be able to impact the individual with what is being presented. This feature is a foremost element is the task of reaching the end customer's attention successfully and beneficially. Thus every aspect of the foray should be carefully explored in order to provide the important information that would be able to cause the desired impact in the targeted audience lives.

Have A Look

The importance of understanding this process is to effectively eliminate any wastage of effort and resources on wrong perceptions made. Understanding the difference between the actual needs of the target audience and measuring it against the perceived needs that the seller has been given to understand will help the seller to redefine the product or service to focus on the afore mentioned fact.

Sometimes however such information can be rather difficult to process as the customer themselves may not entirely know what they specifically need or want.

This can be looked upon as an advantage on the part of the seller as it creates the opportunity for the seller to promote the product or service in a way that is attractive to the customer.

Also when the customer's needs are clearly understood, there can then be a clearer method used to garner the interest and possible successful sale. Advertising and information can be specifically designed to attract the customer based on the information learnt.

Continuously adapting to the customer's interests will allow for the success rates to be better in ensuring the loyalty factor. This in itself can contribute further in creating the customer's faith in the product or service being offered; as it portrays the commitment levels the company is willing to take to ensure the customer stays happy.

All these points are designed to address the customer's needs and interests.

Using the lead generation tool to create a lasting impact on people's lives would without a doubt benefit both the sender and recipient without coming across as being badgering.

When a product or service is being introduced to the target audience the idea is to create a lasting impression form the very onset of the introduction. If this important element is not achieved from the very beginning the rest of the battle to gain the interest and attention of the potential customer is going to be very hard indeed.

Through research, identifying the elements that would create the desired impact on people's lives is not only possible but prudent on the part of the business owner.

Taking the trouble to provide information and even testimonials on the indented item that is being presented is perhaps among the best ways to garner the desired impact on the potential customer's life.

Using notable figures is often encouraged; the element of credibility of such choices should not be underestimated. Beside this, the design of the whole campaign to reach the attention of the potential customer should done in a fashion that leaves the lasting impression that creates the necessary impact to encourage the targeted customer to make a commitment towards an eventual purchase.

The campaign should at all times ensure the impact made is of a positive nature as this will eventually translate to a level of loyalty that cannot be bought.

Chapter 4:

Make Sure To Network

Synopsis

Any field or venture requires some level of networking in order to be more recognizable. Thus the exercise of networking is unavoidable if one wants to be visible and accepted within the framework of one's daily life endeavors. Though most people may look upon the whole exercise of networking as a rather stressful but necessary ingredient of ensuring success there are some tricks than can be used to overcome this mind set.

Networking

Perhaps the best recommended place to start the networking exercise is within the circle of already available friends and business contacts. Learning to constantly network within this environment will then allow the individual to properly practice the much needed skill to ensure the whole experience becomes easier and better, thus further fine tuning the skills needed to be impactful without appearing pushy and off putting.

Another positive feature that can be derived from constantly networking within this environment is that when it is overly done those on the receiving end are more likely to be forthcoming with their well placed advice.

Once comfortable within this environment then the individual should try to expand the networking exercise to include a wider circle of contacts which may not be known to the individual at all. Networking on a wider platform will then ensure the necessary new exposure that can be gained at this level.

Using the internet for expanding online networks is one way to achieve this, as encouraging new contacts will prove useful in the desire to expand one's network portfolio.

At the beginning of trying to establish a relationship online the individual will be able to exercise more confidence as the scenario will be without actually having to face the individual in person, thus making the networking attempt more relaxed. Learning to make it a habit to constantly use every opportunity to expand one's contact list through networking is a trait that should be encouraged.

Chapter 5:
Overhauling Your Property

Synopsis

Most businesses today offer very similar products or services, thus the few ways and individual can ensure an edge over his or her competitors is to strive to provide exceptional customer service.

To work effectively and for one common goal within the company it is very important for all involved to share the same vision. This vision should be clearly defined so that all involved understand the direction in which the company envisions for its product or service, as this makes it easier for all to reach the clearly defined goals reflected through the unified vision.

Changing It

Products today don't really vary too much in terms of functions and price ranges, thus by taking the trouble to provide good customer services the potential customer can be persuaded to consider making repeat purchases.

Below are just some recommendations one can follow in the quest to provide exceptional customer services:

• As most initial enquiries are done over the phone, making it a habit to return or respond to all phone communications is very important and definitely advisable. Doing so in a prompt manner is also another way of making the customer feel important.

• Providing a follow up service or enquiry into the satisfaction of the product or service help both parties gain vital information and builds a relationship of trust and commitment. This also allows the individual an insight to the expectations of the customer.

• Being committed enough to go the extra "mile" is another very important and positive feature in practice. Customers are often put off by this clearly diminishing quality and when extended, the customer will definitely be adequately impressed.

• Taking the customer's concerns seriously and implementing the necessary steps to address these concerns is also another beneficial trait of exceptional customer service. This not only relieves the customers concerns but also establishes the company's commitment to the customer satisfaction guarantee.

• Though sometimes very difficult indeed, there is a very important need to stay focused and view the problem from the customer's perspective. When confronted with a problem a customer can more often than not make unrealistic claims and remarks, thus having a calm demeanor would help to defuse any potentially unpleasant situation.

Having a leadership role or any role within the workings of the company where the vision is clearly outlined and accepted allows for the creation of a set of successful and effective action plan, belief system, values and goals ratio.

Having a clearly defined and powerful vision for the company and ensuring it is completely followed and reflected by all, helps to encourage everyone to incorporate the said vision into their everyday work life to produce the desired positive results.

These visions should be well thought out and appealing to further cultivate the feeling of comradeship and oneness in belonging to something bigger and better than one's own self. It is also what helps to drive everyone to reach their best potential achievements because of the excitement it generates.

When visions are clearly defined by the organization's direction and purpose it should help to inspire loyalty and caring attitudes, which will be displayed and reflected in the unique strengths, that brings about the positive attributes of enthusiasm, belief and commitment of the excited employees

Wrapping Up

As the world of accessing information is ever changing all other related means of technology is also constantly evolving. Sometimes these evolutions happen so fast that people are most often unable to keep abreast with the changes. However it is very important to make a conscious effort to at least try to be in the know.

Though daunting, it can be done with a little effort and interest. One of the reasons it is very important to stay abreast with the latest technology is to ensure one is perceived to be well informed of the developments and to appear knowledgeable and current, thus creating a level of respect within and around peers. The following are some recommendation on how one may attempt to go about doing so.

Though some may avoid using this method for fear of seeming unintelligent, talking to friends, co-workers or anyone who may be well versed with the latest developments in the technological world of gadgets and gizmos is definitely advantageous. Even if one is not very technologically savvy, there will be bits of information that can be acquired through the course of the conversation and by constantly trying to learn more the individual is bound to eventually understand better.

Using the media to access the latest on the technological world is also another way to ensure one is technically knowledgeable. As this is the best form of bringing the latest products to the attention of the general public paying special attention of new reports and features on these topic will allow the individual to gain at the very least a fairly basic level of information on the said products.

Accessing such information on the internet, through technology magazines, browsing bookstores and newsstands is also beneficial towards the quest to stay abreast in the technological world.

Visions for the company can help each individual to challenge themselves to reach higher and previously unthought-of goals. Through the formation of appropriate visions for the company it is also hoped that those involved will feel a sense of importance and appreciation and thus continue to strive to do their best both for the company and for themselves.

www.ingramcontent.com/pod-product-compliance
Lightning Source LLC
Chambersburg PA
CBHW021449170526
45164CB00001B/444